Unbound: Poems 2022-2023

Tarh Martha Ako Mfortem

Hafan Books

Published by Hafan Books, 2023

ISBN 978-1-7384049-0-2

© Tarh Martha Ako Mfortem, 2023. All rights reserved.

Design: Tom Cheesman

Hafan Books is a project of Swansea Asylum Seekers Support

All proceeds go to the charity

www.sass.wales

c/o PeoplePlus, 30 Orchard St, Swansea SA1 5AT

Contents

Introduction by Eric Ngalle Charles 5
Acknowledgements 7

No Price for Peace – Refugee Songs
Sanctuary Seekers 8 Unbound 11 Asylum Hike 13
Boat of Destiny 15 Refugee 17

A Vicious Cycle – Laments for Africa
Hearken to My Pleas 19 A Requiem for Africa 20
Conscienceless 22 Merchants of Doom 23
French Africa 26 Of Legends and Posterity 27
Dead Glories 29 Candle in Distress 30

To Take on Generations – Women's Chorus
His Strikes 32 Mortal Man 34 When It Is Enough 35
Woman Magic 36 The African Woman 37
A Mother's Dance 40 A Widow's Song 42

My Bed is Cold – Tunes for ...
Only You 44 Without You 45
Phone Call in the Rain 47 Love-struck 49

The Earth Weeps – Nature Elegies
Sip by the Ocean 52 Lumin Illuminates 54
Light in the Tunnel 56 Alas! the Raven Trips 58
Bonds of the Atlantic 60

Still in Nightmares Roses Bloom – Verses for Wales
Dylan Sleeps 62 Rhossili Blues 63
Talybont-on-Usk Tallies 65 Sassy SASS 67
Time to Change Wales 70 Swansea City of Sanctuary 72

When Trees Fall on Trees – Closing Chords
The Fronts Bend 76 Burst Bubbles 78
When Trees Fall on Trees 79 If Love Were Human... 80

Introduction

Eric Ngalle Charles

A ship caught in a tidal storm of despair: this is how I felt, feasting my senses as I read through this gem of a collection. These poems will slice through your deepest fears and lay them bare. Talk about setting the place on fire. It's a bendigedig* collection. As a reader, sometimes it takes me a while to get hooked on a new writer. However, Martha's poems and their integrity shine throughout, and they catch you from the start, leaving no room for manoeuvre. Like many other African writers now, Martha's poetry is like a resurrection, a literary ogbanje**, a spirit child bringing to light the plight of Africans who have grown up burdened with our history and our colonial past, divided along inherited lines of cultures and languages alien to us. Ours will not be a generation of meaningless history! The poems in this collection warn those potbelly men who have adopted the settler's position, bleeding the country dry. We are on the march and we will throw stones at your glass houses until everyone has their fair share of the national cake!

bendigedig – in Welsh: fantastic, brilliant.

**ogbanje* – in Igbo: a spirit child who causes calamity; "the voice that comes and bites; the worse you can do is kill us; we return in multiples, and stronger" (ENC). See Ben Okri's novel, *The Famished Road* (1991).

Acknowledgements

I would like to acknowledge with gratitude the unconditional support of my friends in all the organisations I volunteer at in Swansea, especially Steve Pullinger of the Friends and Neighbours charity, Tom Cheesman at Hafan Books, David Jones of the People's Library, and everyone at Swansea Asylum Seekers Support.

Special gratitude goes to my beautiful daughters: Muriel, Skyla, Cindy and Zahara for their support and love. They keep me going and this collection would not have been possible without them.

No Price for Peace: Refugee Songs

Sanctuary Seekers

My land became my enemy
When the footstool of my ancestors
Lay beaten to dust
And terror, war and crime
Deprive me of my voice

I beseech the powerful
To wreak no havoc
For in my frustration
I have no option
But to watch them cry and hail

The sounds so strange
That reap life
As I watch many fall
For no crime of theirs

My land bleeds
My siblings weep
Our once cherished altars
Now haunt our gods

What is our crime?
I have toiled in peace
I have reaped a barnful
But today I beg
From the dregs of my land

Where did we go wrong?
As the guns sound endlessly
I carve my niche
And sail my craft

The waters I have tested
And death I have crushed
My life was on the line
As I gasped for a chance

The ocean scares me not
In my sojourn undefined
Where to, is the question
As the rowing boat founders

I leave to weep for my land
A once emblematic kingdom
I leave with regrets
With tribulations huge

No jacket, no paddle, no food
As I surrender to nature
I cannot remember my name
My troubles have erased my mind

I cannot tell my age
The numbers all seem strange
I am resigned to fate
As I yearn for peace

I long to tell my travails
And the risks I have taken
Lo! today my tale is new
In a strange, beautiful land

A sanctuary so warm
That I reject my pains
And welcome a new lifestyle
In a city unknown to my clan
Where today I tell my tale

In appreciation of my fortress
Be sung a song of praise
By all and sundry
To celebrate my life
My journey and my pains

Unbound

When the crows at dawn
Resonate in wails
That my ancestry be bloody
And my life be threaded
To quit a dungeon
Amidst such chaos
The failure of ego
Becomes a trophy to warlords

My life, a nightmare
My nation, a fiend
The melody unchanging
And a future so bleak

Today's blessings bend
Away from the madding wails
And deafening blasts
Away from mortality
I sought refuge in a sanctuary
A tale anew and yet
Worries lingering

My tale, my strength to overcome
The past, but it still haunts
For the rhythm's unchanged
For the world is sick

In this fortress, an olive branch
The best versions of humanity

Arms wide to cuddle
Sharing in warmth
The greatest gifts of life
Love so immeasurable
For there's no price for peace

A home anew, a future of hope
A sanctuary still unfolds
A blessing to serve and be served
To yearn and learn
For only a city of sanctuary
Can give such peace

Asylum Hike

May this bolthole
Not bring peril
In my quest
No olive branch be broken

Through the dungeon
Nightmares resurface
I trod in horror
Peace I seek

In this stronghold
My anguish is rekindled
Threats and hate
Still come unsolicited

Nostalgia steams in me
My identity a question
To wait, the journey
And to hope, the goal

Succumbed to bleakness
A future perplexing
When lives hang
On the thinnest thread

The wait is draining
The ache is enormous
My pillow knows my tale
For the nights are long

My nation bequeathed me
A task to overcome
Unforeseen future
Desperate steps

I hope to smile at last
From a harrowing loop

Boat of Destiny

In the raging storm
The mood so low
A flapping sail
Still tears the heart

The horizon unseen
And snares of doom
That frenzy afloat
The risk to sail

When anguish looms
And self-reflection is lost
To hope is all
A journey unfolds

The stillness of the night
And flapping of the waters
That cursed reality
Of life on a noose

Where thoughts go wild
What prayer resounds
Where pain rebounds
To perish is no tune

For escape is key
And the future so bleak
When nightmares surface

To venture is to curse

With no safety measures
Nor itinerary known
No tale of fun
For they that dare

No age assigned
No gender defined
On this expedition
The sailor is self

Lo! the grumbling of the waves
The dance of the boat
The music of flapping waters
And singing seagulls

The raging ocean
And endless waves
The clinging and hugging
The fears and phobias

The surrender to nature
The stripping of man
The gain and the pain
Eclipse the threat

Refugee

In my wilderness of thoughts
My tale rebounds

My toes have tasted rocks
My eyes have seen my ears
And my feet have seen the earth
In my homeland, my fortress
Where the music so familiar
Was long so forlorn

Today I stand estranged
Banished and ejected
From my own very essence
I, that the arms crafted
Close to death's stir

In my fatherland
This sting shook my brain
This blade shaved my head
This ammunition of reminiscence
Pushed me to an alien
And pushed aside my treasures

Today I seek a fortress
And peace so priceless
In a globe so unknown

Today the sun refused to set
And my shadow became so shy

That it shrinks to my soles
For I challenged myself to live

I am a jungle product
Where freshness and nature roam
Today I turn a new leaf
Miles from my navel stalk

Miles from my fountain
To imbibe afresh a culture
A way and a lifestyle
Anew in all ramifications

I throw myself into this hurricane
To direct my thoughts and actions
I submit to nature
To be smitten in its furnace
And induce in me finesse
To embrace mankind
The odds and the evens
For my gratitude is boundless

With the warmest embraces
I feel home away from home
Life remains a challenge
This world is not for the frail
Yet the edges gather for us all

A Vicious Cycle: Laments for Africa

Hearken to My Pleas

Drunken monster
You dead bulbs
With frozen thoughts
All bleeding thugs
Confiscated memories
Corrugated minds
Jigsaw puzzles
In crooked boxes
Hideous cultures
Abridged versions
Frustrated ventures
In dark closets
Deranged experts
Test primitive novices
Corrupt farmers
Hire blunt sickles
Who is the mentor?
Who Is the quack?
A vicious cycle
Chased by the weak
The meek and the bloated
And awaken to wail
Trials at dusk
The world unknown

A Requiem for Africa

Where inconsistency wallows
Kinfolk sink in false progress as sucklers of filth
In the dusty plains, valleys and plateaus
Where the remnants of war, poverty
Corruption, disease and tyranny lie
Amidst the frustrations of generations
And the ever-stretchy apron strings of colonialism

Where the dregs of humanity suffer
Demonisation by earthly rulers
Principalities and powers in self-proclaimed authority
Where jungle justice prevails and equity is a sham
The gifts of nature are looted and wasted
In the face of starving generations of the wealthiest continent
And the unborn are blessed with inherited debts

The proud tyrants' arrogant greed
Knows no bounds in their evil choices
For in the fine lines of nature and divinity
A rebirth is a paramount fallacy

Mankind is limited and even they that birth the wise
In this foolery of means and ways
Still stay true to the biased nature of existence
As they drown in their limitations and lust

Mankind slumbers with no vessels of hope
In this glaring horizon they are still blind to see
But chant great melancholic strains

While their masses cheer in famine and thirst

Their crooked voices echo their evil and drollness
And revert in resonance amidst cries of the hopeless homeless
Their brains are as archaic as their thoughts
As their pocket politics is highlighted in shameless exhibits

These clueless rebels reap in abundance
And watch their seeds squander their loot
While they lie back to host the buffoonery of their mentors
That repel judgements of the unjust in arrogance

Forcefully blinking calamities as they tred
Life is a monster to them that await in awe
Singing dirges and eulogies for requiems
Their fall would be as mighty as their deeds
And their tales would be sung by generations
But surely, rebirth is a constant

Conscienceless

Hell broke loose
At the feet of the sorcerer
When the thirst so long-lasting
Was quenched by smiting
All the heartless despots
That reap carcasses
Bleating by the clock
As the echoes drop

This once outstanding puritan
And product of jigsaw nightmares
Stares dumbfounded
As fountains force
The earth to twist

Had the martyr not leapt
At this fundamental anguish
This throbbing might be doomed
In absolute power and tyranny
To cast down the populace

Merchants of Doom

Never again, merchants of doom
Mankind as cargo to expedite
Never again, gold raiders
The betrayals endured
Enough of this barter
Where strength is jewel
Auctioned as the lamb

No price for peace
Forcefully captured and jailed
The greed in our blood
Coastal raiders a thorn of a tale
Transatlantic violators
Looters preening

Stripped of humanity
Dumped as filth
For the natural selection
Your death a prize

Who is to blame?
All hands are soiled
Even the harsh tropical weather
Even the forests resisted
Even nature rebelled
Reduced to baselessness
Stripped of humanity
Abused by fortune makers
Fought over for supremacy

Man's evil to man
Who will pay the price?
Who will unturn the red pages?
Those rusted chains continue to wail
The cries and echoes
Still haunt

Sitting shackled for months
The hopes and fears of mutiny
The struggles of liberators
The redness of the Atlantic Ocean
The sharks trailing the jettisoned
The shame of blood

Man's insatiable quests
For economic dominance
Dehumanised by conquistadors
Brutalised and sexually abused
Speechless and blindfolded

The blood of liberators
The might of the struggles
Gone with the winds
These incredible atrocities
That yet go unpunished
This pain of generations
That no amends can dull

In this caricature
Lie the remnants of nature

Rob not their glories
Nor question their furies
For when wealth is the key
Death is the fee

All live in hope
In this scary globe
And none is immortal
Within this portal

French Africa

Thugs in colonial garments parade the mines and shores
Outnumbered in wit but fuelled to loot and destroy

These apron strings stay so strong
Where deceit reigns you are condemned to toil
For crumbs on your own soil

Your leaders seem doomed, outskilled in gimmicks
Ruled by the hoaxes of crooked masters of doom

Your students wallow in dullness and regrets
Cursed to the bones to creep where others walk
Reduced to beggars in a land of plenty

Who did curse you? Who ordained your fears?
Who keyed your lips? Why
Must you throw your gems to dogs?

Doff not your caps to these ancestral mind-games
Listen not to archaic lectures
Give no dime unjustly
Claim what you sowed for the future

Sleep no more, denizens
Reclaim your rights and lands
Be the voice of generations
The smiths who forge the key to freedom

Of Legends and Posterity

The high barricades of flamboyant castles
And the huge and stiff walls of treachery
Hide the sleepless and noisy fountains
Of monsters beating soundless drums
Murmuring in chaos
Likened to earthly mammoths
Adorned in celestial habits

They refuse to hearken to the pleas and wails
Of the downtrodden and scathed
Who are made to cower by agents of doom
Muckers, tyrants and demagogues

Renowned fraudsters parade the corridors of power
In sophisticated costumes and regalia
Their hearts of steel know no pain or regrets
As they waste their lives on chess boards
Sipping the finest wines around the best damsels
Smashing their feeders at their convenience
And mocking at their lurking folks

What a waste it is to be led by the inefficient
And supposedly entrenched capitalists
Who brag and preach of democracy

They are self-proclaimed African kings
Groomed to display cowardice in palaces
And soak their shameless heads in their sweaty cassocks

These colonial stalkers get cynical and physical
They reap where they never sowed
They loathe the archaic whistle sounds
That crack the walls of truth
And the chant of doomsday
That unveils their undivine and obscured lives

In the dungeons they shall dance
To the confused sounds of gongs
And in their nightmares
Watch the cherubins display

Though their secrets
May be as deep as the ocean
A man shall never be late
For his own death

Dead Glories

We roam at dawn in quest of nightmares
Soliloquizing at noon and creeping at dusk

Like fugitives we flee
As we raise the dust on our shadows

No haven is nigh in our quest for glory
Lost dreams long forgotten

In our bid for peace we wailed on warpaths
That monsters trod amidst all raging storms

No heart yearns for fame where drought resides
None can light the lantern where sadness abounds

Tales are long forgotten of martyrs and their songs
Were it not for humanity many would chain the dead

We shall watch you fall
We shall sing to your demise
All our shattered pieces
Shall again be made whole

You cannot take a piece
Of all you worked to destroy
You shall not dine forever
On the tables of the downtrodden

Candle in Distress

Brighten a gloomy soul today
For we all are obligated
To relinquish our widow's mite
To be a lit candle for humanity

Generations are in hunger and dearth
The environment and climate are raging
Many are victims of wars and plagues
Bodies are warped by pains and aches

Annihilated by life's struggles
And invisible chains
Damned and doomed
To fantasise of divine remedies

Thirsting for change
Is the dream of millions
Who were born in anguish
To die in abject poverty

Heal our world
Stretch a hand
Touch on lives in agony
Eschew all forms of violence of the past

All that are divinely blessed
Should sit not on their blessings
The secret of receiving
Is in imparting

That the lord loves a cheerful giver
Is truly scriptural
Giving is a virtue and a ministry
We all are blessed to earn and donate

A hungry man is an angry man
Extinguish poverty and celebrate peace
Give richly and wisely what your life depends on
Donate unconditionally to everyone in need

Let colour, race, age, and distance not define our freewill
Count your blessings and reap folds of replenishment
Be the hand of change to our sick and sad world
That we shall not be late to save a soul

We are all sculpted in celestial imagery
And our divine self chases love and simplicity
Love is the greatest and everlasting virtue
We shall reap what we sow

To Take on Generations: Women's Chorus

His Strikes

In the heart of the day
When the leaves grow thin
I will look to the skies
And ponder on life

I met him in smiles
I tore myself to bits
The look so fierce haunts
As he throws the grip on me

The struggles were profound
And our love was more
But those blows invoke
That demon uncast in him

Still I tear up and bear up
In my hope to redeem
This creature of darkness
That seems to dim my light

In his frustrations I share
My life is yoked to his beat
Hell knows my tales
When the strikes burst

My flesh was devoured
In his quest for morality

I was subjected to pain
Hell knows my tales

I shall pause to revive
All my lost glories
Though it wrecks
My existence

No key to violence shall prevail
Let no mortal be a drum
Let not marriage be a storm
And man the drummer

Mortal Man

This caricatured stump
Yelling and crawling on filth
Boasting in arrogance
Demonized to toil
With critical consequences
Whose goal is undefined
Retreats and retraces
Same daily steps chasing oblivion

Sizzling in seasons
Deformed in wit and faculty
Messy from womb to tomb
Reformed to plod and quest
Amassing dirt to dust
Declined in means and prowess
Yet resonates in nightmares
Hosting and boasting

Then will zoom in once
Condemned to stillness
With no future or destiny
Subject to mortality
And quests abandoned
In cold chilliness
With no visible footprints
But the shadows of rapacity

When It Is Enough

Walking the idle paths of life
Where fists fumble and fondle
Clueless and illiberal
While dishonesty chases the mighty
The ubiquitous yearning
On the lecher's footstool
As on the hassock they revere

The roamer like a bee
Sucks from every debutante
And sniffs on loose lingerie
Chastising their patsy

No bouquet toss to remember
Yet debunked by the beau monde
The cleavages have seen it all
Not a single tale remains unknown or untold
Of the spoony with truncated lifestyle
And of monster man and fallen soldiers
Hustling and pulling down the meek
And draining their little tanks in every vessel

Then, flees for good to later soliloquize
We have painted them red

Like butterflies they must shield in cocoons awhile
The withered remnants of subterfuge by the libidinous

Woman Magic

When genders test their worth
One stands mighty
Procreation was always key

Known to be humble and brave
The hymns of deceit abound
As in her meekness she toils
Yet society frowns

To take on generations
A Herculean task
Sacrificing monthly gains
In pain she wastes herself
In the wrinkles of motherhood

Blessed in a cursed abode
She toils and smiles
Miseries and patience locked to position
Keeper of the mystery to seal her lips and bow

Her bravery opens all blocked doors
Champions development
Recognising her services and her need
To make the world habitable to all

This is the magic of a woman
Frailty is not woman!

The African Woman

Dark as the continent
Your world has known no joy
You are magic and mystery
In your world

Your flesh has tasted hardship and disease
As your limbs toil from morning to night
Like the ant you never complain
For suffering is the song of your days

You are breadwinner and carer
Down generations, your story is the same
Your unscripted and untold plight
Is the chorus in the rain and sun

Your blood has always been hot
As you fend for your children
No kitchen magic beats your skills
In your quest to make ends meet

Your woes are endless
Your woes stretch unlimited
Your pains have been your gain
In pregnancy and in childbirth

Your strength cannot be questioned
In the grumbling of your stomach
Your environs show no remorse
As you are early to rise and late to rest

The stones have known the soles of your feet
And darkness has become your friend
Though your soul longs for the best of life
Your refrain has never been the better

Yawning and cuddling, starving and thirsty
You turn the hands of the clock
You are the mother, wife and daughter
Who murders sleep to make ends meet

You are the author of the best lullabies
And the best voice to your offspring
You are the deprived illiterate
And teenage mother

You are the trader, teacher and babysitter
Who relies on her own shoulders for a nap
You are the politician
And lawmaker barefoot

You are the victim of famine
Drought and malnutrition
With milkless breasts
You try to feed your offspring

The Harmattan has counted your bones
Your ribs have seen your flesh
Deep cracks and sores on your limbs
Have made the fly your friend

Steadfast in your pains and cramps
Sharing all your life depends on
Your sacrifices pass unacknowledged
Warrior, toiling in the heat, baby on your back

Your age-old symbol, breastfeeding skeleton
Must never define you
For no crime of yours
The world has turned its back against you

Your leaders have eaten corruption
And shamelessly parade their faces
You are the victim of bad governance
And the product of deranged rulers

Biases and invisible chains
And warlords have defined you
This must someday
Give way to a new dawn

A Mother's Dance

Old lullabies renewed on tired tongues
When unending tantrums surface
This tired chest knows no rest
Dancing to the tune of wailing

Enduring and smiling at her reasonable task
She will not lie or rest till nature forces her
Yawning and swaying to her beautiful tune
Her love must keep her stronger

In ecstasy and pain she reaps
That confidence which pushes her to sway
Just to sooth the witching hours
And pacify the little heavy eyes and legs

Even in her sleep she keeps her watch
This ingenious skill she alone possesses
A unique gift that goes unnoticed
Her own invisible trophy

Her job is as endless as the straps on her back
Her chest and back are for naps and cuddles
Nothing compares to this warmth and feeling
To the neonate and the toddler

Being close to breasts, milk and her warmth
Being rocked in the arms and a head on the heart
Listening to soft lullabies
The cries are never too much

Even in the heart of the night
She is a drug to the restless
She does not care who watches or who hates
Some awful sounds that keep the neighbours awake

Comes a quarrel in the morning
Her enemies increase
Her woes multiply but still
Her cuddles and dances are her only focus

A quiet nap
Is all she longs for
Nap time is here!
She sighs with relief

A Widow's Song

My lost glories are haunting
My tribulations are at a peak
I cannot turn back the hands of time
Or restore my stolen treasures

To forge ahead is my desire
Though the world makes a mockery of me
Today they bite my fingers
These fingers that fed them

I have become an outcast
And a stranger in my home
My offspring wanders
In the cracks of the universe

Yet I shall not dwell on provocations
Or kill the dreams I built
The future is only bleak
To those that make it so

I was not tailored for crumbs
But life has given my fair share
I toil from dawn to dusk
When once I reigned in affluence

My enemies have reaped my sweat
And laugh as I deteriorate
I must weather this storm
I have known love and hate

My bones must not capitulate
To fleshly desires and hurts
My poverty is for all to see
But my glories reflect in my offspring

The weather is now my friend as I labour
My hands have touched the worst of filth
My brightness has turned to grey
But I shall not complain

I have seen the true colours of mankind
I have watched the different shades of torture
And I have developed a cocoon
To repel life's daggers and arrows

My rights and privileges have been seized
The world has ridiculed, cursed and stoned me
When prayers are my meals, faith keeps me going
Much sweat has gone down the drain

Tough times must come to an end
Where hope and work dwell
Tomorrow's songs shall sound very different
To the ears of the vicious

The future is bright and fruitful
I shall not complain but reap from all my toil
And put the world to shame
Mankind is most true when pain is most high

My Bed is Cold: Tunes for ...

Only You

My thoughts are full of you
All I crave is you
My heart beats fast for you
Maybe racing for you
I blindly yearn for you
As all my thoughts of you
Are that I long for you
And hope to make of you
A diamond effigy of you
A great replica of you
In all my cravings for you
And all my quests for you
I see the light in you
For you are you and you
Alone I must uphold you
In this mystery of you
Is my mastery of you
In endless thoughts of you
My feelings magnify you
And none can ever be you
When you are not you
None is close to you
As none is fair to you
For you are you and you
And this tale tells all of you

Without You

Without you
The nights are cold and long

My dreams are nightmares
I have scribbled unending images of you
My bin is full of papers

I miss those hugs and cuddles
Those long and wet kisses
The little midnight games we played
Our constant little fights

All my thoughts are full of you
My pillow is wet all night
Nothing means a thing to me
Your absence is killing me

I drink myself to a stupor
Trying to forget the past
Haunted by your silhouette
Craving for your grasp
Your palm in mine was a mystery

I miss those warm moments
When you sang into my ears
Your breath so warm
As you whistled the soft words

My heart melted when

You called my pet name
Those midnight whispers and jokes
I long for those caresses
That hurt but soothe

Life is empty and my bed is cold

Those moonlight beach stories
The night baths in the rivers
Our hunting expeditions
Old tales by the fireside
Breakfast in bed

When you swept me off my feet
The unending assurance
Of love and protection

By your side my fears are finished
Your breath is magic
Your lap and arm my pillow

This mystery called love

Nothing means a thing to me
Your absence is killing me

Phone Call in the Rain

When the urge to speak surmounts the pain
When you are swept off the ground
By the vibrations of a ringing phone
Or the melody of the best tunes
In ecstasy one recites a tale
The pains of forgone acts

Blown by the love of hearing a voice
And stuck to a phone amidst the storm
No raging tempest is mightier
Where raindrops are music to the ears

Nothing means a thing
Where words and echo marry
No intruder is noticed
When our minds are miles away

The slow but steady steps made
The giggles, frowns and laughter
The reactions of limbs and organs
The feeling of madness to onlookers
While the words like lyrics flow so sweet

The rain denotes the tone of voice
As the sounds of the raindrops
Blend in to the music of the surroundings
When soaked in the flow of sweet conversation
There is much beauty in heedlessness
Especially one from a heart so dear

The kilometres you walk on the same spot
Drenched in unnoticed cold rainwater
Tell of the strength of sounds and waves
And the prowess of water melody

No umbrella can stop love's voice
No storm can control love's waves
No dangers can put love's voice to slumber
No wetness is felt on a phone call
No thunderbolt is bolder than a worried heart
No lightning is brighter and swifter
No scares and scars are noticed

One's lost consciousness
Is lifted by the wavy sounds
As love endures all hurt
Nothing seems so romantic
As a phone call in the rain

Love-struck

I cannot be a shadow
To my truths and weaknesses

I shall not feign happiness
Or smile in my tears

I do not want to explore alone
When my heartbeat is weakest

I need you by my side
To roam the universe

With you my missing rib
The rivers will never run dry

If I must journey alone
The sea would never be breezy

The nights would never be starry
When you are miles away

The moon shall not be bright
When I am trapped indoors

I would not dance alone
When the fireflies crown my head

I need those hugs to sleep
When all is cold and freezing

I cannot live to the fullest
When you only dwell in my thoughts

The sands on the beaches would be rocks
If I walk on the beach alone

I wish to sit on your lap
I wish to lie on your chest

I wish to enjoy those cuddles
That trigger the songs within

I wish to hear those snores
When the nights are warm and long

Allow me to rub and fondle
The muscles I had known

May we walk together
To fight and smile forever

Give me a chance to whisper
When the nights are cold and freezing

Release me from my worries
And purge me of this bondage

Sing the lullabies of old
And pet me while I doze

In the comfort of your arms
I wish to come of age

Speak peace upon my being
And convert me to be yours

I wish to learn to live and love
And explore all of nature

May our frailties not limit us
To put giant footprints on the sands of time

My thoughts of you are haunting
My dreams have turned to nightmares

I feel drowsy and insecure
Do not leave me in the cold

School me in your wit and skills
Teach me not to live alone

When the time to bond is ripe
Let not my wait be eternal

For I shall drink myself to stupor
Lay down my armour

And wave
To our unbalanced world

The Earth Weeps: Nature Elegies

Sip by the Ocean

When the setting sun controls
The night birds' patrol
The horizon reflects
The moody one's refrain

In my loneliness I seek a quench
That my tastebuds deserve
To put a halt to my toiling
As I ponder by the Atlantic

Mixed feelings crop and go
As I sip of my bottle

I claim this liberty
To listen to my bottle sing
As it empties, its music divine
Celebrating nature and freedom

I know no sound this pure
This interaction of nature
That makes a mortal wonder
And pushes me to ponder
The mysteries of life

In my empty bottle a flute
Its music echoing
The smoothness of lyrics

Its language the finest
To my mind

Life in inanimate display
We perceive and swipe
And cluelessly ignore
For we seek superiority
And control of the orb
And pay no heed
To the cries and mourning
Of flora and fauna

Look well and redeem
Those hurtful tolls
That bleed nature
And place a curse on us

Lumin Illuminates

The freshness of the mornings
And beauty of shades
Great gift of Mother Nature
For mankind to behold

Our orb, a gift to preserve
To respect and on departing
Hand down through generations
Our duty to protect

Our vow to Mother Earth
Our oath to heal
Mankind betrays today
In greed and ignorance

Our planet is in transition
Abuse is our tune
Man in his hopelessness
Has devoured the roots

Today the earth weeps
As seasons grey in decay
All that nature tailored to bloom
The finest tastes of life

Bursts of recipes
Meant to savour buds
Lost exploration of flavours
The bare necessities of life

Flora and fauna
Struggle for survival
Where invisible harsh blades
Chop life off the buds

Mankind now hopeless and vain
Wanders in thirst and hunger
The recipe for healing
Resides in our being

Stop the abuse of Mother Earth
Learn of our responsibility
Our duty to the ecosystem
Our conscience to judge

Light in the Tunnel

My shadow fades away
As the firefly dances on my head
Moonlight tunes abound
In the chaos of echoes

The refrain is same
The loggers insane
Whose tunes are new
For I am breathless

My habitat a sham
The liberties of steel
Invaders of jungles
Heartless to the core

Age old bonds destroyed
The owl on my roof
The cuckoo's strain
Silenced at dusk

The mammoth in tears
Bows to ignorance
A once ancient whistle
Drained and blown

Tomorrow's melodies gone
In this rubble and ramble
The voice of wisdom doomed
Forever to weep in vain

Your metropolis in ruins
Reduced to natural disasters
Still in this calamity
The drive unreversed

The time is ripe
To clean our planet
To save the woods
And heal the world

Alas! the Raven Trips

Alas! the raven trips
On the rugged web
The artist in awe resigns
As the woodpecker's tunes
Emblem the woods

The smiling ranunculus stirs
As the dewy rosy petals bloom
This melody of old
Which summertime reveres

Fuming perfume smells
Fill the environs
As gentle flavours are savoured
By the smooth and the rugged

Nobody betters the softness
Of these background melodies
That push the wailing to slumber
And the travellers to rest

Yet the friar dreams
Of a world of imagination
Of the fairest and finest
This visionary pilgrim mourns
A diluted universe
Where the sky reflects
The sorrows of the days

As moody man
Heaves sighs of relief
Amidst limb struggles
And terrestrial cravings

In this piteous state
All are cursed to strive
In quest of better livelihood

Bonds of the Atlantic

Racing cans and bottles
Dance to the wavy rhythms
Of waves flapping with filth

Seagulls parade to the tunes of the tides
Twerking fishes float and strolling crabs burrow
Through the grumbling and thunderous waves

The shells on the sands
The network of crab holes
The smoothness of beach stones
The fineness of the sand
The might of beach rocks
Paint the beautiful glamour of the Atlantic

The stratus mirrors the sea
As the horizon is a puzzle

The rejected of the sea
The dumpings on the shores
The angry transport of waste
The roaring of the waters
To the anger of the waves
The music of flapping tides
The might of the sea
Mirror the strength of the waters

For the sea is friend and fiend
Its mystery a jungle still unknown

An untamed, uncharted habitat

The breeze makes a spectacle
Of dancing leaves and bubbling dresses
The lifting of litter and flight of objects
The whistling of empty cans and bottles
The clicking and clacking of human things
The singing of metals and glass
The blending of the sounds
Racing in the direction of the breeze

The might and wideness of the sea
Is a mystery teeming with marine life
The parades of legendary sea kings and queens
In a fearless home and raging transporter

The blueness of the wavy waters
Reflects the bright and full moon
And the fading sunrays of dusk

The quiet dance steps of insects in nearby bushes
The tests of strength of animals on trees
The skydiving skills of birds in response to the tides
The serene and gentle dance of sea creatures on the beach
The sounds of worldly music

The barefoot sand strolls
The splashing and puddling of tails and fins
By monsters on sea patrols
Paint the beautiful glamour of the Atlantic

Still in Nightmares Roses Bloom: Verses for Wales

Dylan Sleeps

The poet is asleep
In finest lyric lines
Yearning for a utopian world
Where dreams never fade

The verses of old resonate
Fresh in the hearts of new generations
Still depicting the frustrations
Of man in his strange orb

Born in war to fight the unknown
A world torn by greed and hate
Still in nightmares roses bloom
No bomb can stop a ticking brain

What joy to read his rugged lines
The pure chastity of his thoughts
A short dream that resists the wind
A legacy gargantuan

Rhossili Blues

Where the ocean reflects the sky
And the summer sands are warm
Where the huge sand dunes
Align the green hills
The pink petals glow
And the waters are so cold
And the breeze so endless
That each soul refreshes

Here the flora's tunes
Mellow the fauna's steps
On the sandy footpaths
Here tanning is restful
Where the nests and mats are anchored
For the basking and the healing

Surfers and swimmers awake
To this endless stretch of nature
To its sounds, smells and beauty
From sunrise to sunset
This self-cleansing mammoth
Whose flotsam and jetsam
Regurgitate its debris
Right on the beach steps
Dead crabs, jelly fish and more
Shells of all sizes and shapes
Strange carcasses of aquatic creatures
That leave the common man in awe

This great touristic bed
That heals the body, mind and soul
That mends the broken-hearted
And strengthens the meek and downtrodden
This love rekindler
That opens its doors to all
A hotspot for visitors
Who come to rejuvenate
Away from the madding cities

This healing vessel
With the widest salty waters
And mysterious aquatic life
These fine and soft beach sands
Where visitors can sip and bite
And dine with the seagulls

This yet unmimicked melody
That sways all linens and fabrics
Of the young and the old
And grabs a dance or a fall
To the tune of the sea breeze
This strength of nature
And of abandoned derelict vessels

Our world remains a mystery
Which man is still to unravel
A nod we do not understand

Talybont-on-Usk Tallies

Dedicated to the good folk of
Hay Brecon Talgarth Sanctuary for Refugees
June 2023

Capturing the sights and sounds of nature
Talybont was good to us
This ever green neighbourhood
Adorned with the finest sights
Great archives of past travels
Serene vegetation, calm waters and relief features
A wealth of flora and fauna
Most colourful petals and buds

Outstanding in colonial trade
Remnants of industrial ties
The fine lyrics of Vaughan
Horse tracks and bridges of old
Steam locomotive train lines
Relics of the mighty coal lords
Still this silence resonates
With unique history

The canal so cool and legendary
Spans millennia with still water channels
This mighty travel line millions boarded
Home to beautiful indigenes
Highlife resort to peace lovers
Business line to marketers
And friend to solo voyagers

Dishing out capital, love and romance
To lovers, merchants and tourists
And to lover ducks and ducklings

Green fields well shaped
Pruned trees of competing heights
Here serenity is key
A breathtaking scenario
Peaceful landscape
Green grazing for fauna
Beautiful and gentle hills
And valleys so cool

The tally of Talybont cuisines
Is second to none
Fresh finest flavours and tastes
The savouring was incessant
Flamboyant in style and manner
With veg of all colours
Salads and desserts
A jam of cakes and icings
Irresistible colours
Classy menu for all and sundry
For salivating mouths
The taste of the pudding
Was in the eating

Sassy SASS

Dedicated to the good folk of
Swansea Asylum Seekers Support

Engulfed in our meekness we all
Strive to redeem our lost glories and pain
Dark shades and memories
Pull us to converge, to heal and to share in dining

We share the fruits of mankind
And feel so honoured
That each day's lightning
Brings forth a rainbow

We all hope and dream for the best
As we share our challenges and struggles
In our welcoming symposium
We talk and learn

We share our successes and tribulations
We forget our past pain
For the mysteries of life
Are never evenly foretold

We never regret our bold steps
As we stare at bold faces with hope
Feeling fulfilled and safe
In our home away from home

SASS is that abode

Where chains of frustration are broken
Where the miserable find love
Where the lonely meet peers
Where humanity is revered
And life is priceless

We feel this unimaginable warmth
That each week we crave to converge
We play, learn and eat together
We receive gifts from Samaritans and charities
This great display of love that knows no bounds

We learn to share and care
For sharing is a virtue imbibed in humankind
Which even the young acknowledge

We are grateful for this timeless initiative
That turns our frowns to laughter
That consoles us endlessly
When all our dreams seemed to fade away

SASS gives hope to the hopeless
A haven to the frustrated
We cannot express enough gratitude
For this selfless initiative where staff toil relentlessly
To put smiles on our wrinkled faces and torn lives

Today we can smile again
We can interact and showcase our talents
Proving that we are not tabula rasa
For we journeyed with our skills and culture

We can impact our community
And strive for the best in our new kingdom

May the doors of our fortress lie open to us
As we outpour the best of ourselves

We pray for SASS to grow
Incorporating more social activities
Encouraging more skills development
We long for more translators at our symposium
More outdoor events to help us discover our country
More recreational activities to boost our mental health
Opportunities to showcase our acting skills
We long to tell our stories in a movie
For our life is our tale

Many have been through a furnace
And cheated death severally
Many have passed through the eye of a needle
And have spat on the face of death

We recognise our individual differences
Shades, talents, weaknesses and strengths
Our trajectories may differ
Our pains may be the same
SASS is the shoulder to lean on
SASS is the mother who lays bare her chest
To feed with no discrimination
We remain indebted
To this gargantuan project

Time to Change Wales

*For the charity campaign to end
discrimination and stigma around mental health*

In this wasteland of melancholic strains
The starry skies depict our minds
Profound in miseries but simulating ecstasy
Each point of light reclaims tranquillity

We all reflect anguish and dejection
But we feign love and peace
Condemned to tearful smiles
Restrained in speech and action
All sink in woes and quests
Clad in our soggy mortal robes
Doomed and shaped by life's limitations

Oh! that this orb treats us so
This colossus aweary
Of joys all limited
And worries gruesome
Oh! that we are limited in speech
To count the stars all night

Let our healing source be us
And let our health be our gold
Let's feed our minds and heal our land
That each may live and not merely exist
Or lament and exit prematurely

No island is in mankind
When mental health affects and infects
We all must seek redress
To build strong bonds of unconditional love

Kill the stigmas, cut the double-binds
Supplant discrimination with conversation
Pledge and turn the tables
Tell your tale and break the chains
Be the voice to overhaul your being
Be the new face of change

Healing must begin from you
Put a signature for change
It's time for action
Be the champion

Swansea City of Sanctuary

This sanctum sanctorum of great prodigies
As white as the swans of goodly hue
Home of great legends and birthplace of the munificent
Historic city of Glamorgan, in Welsh Abertawe
This rostrum of the homeless and fortress of the persecuted
This sacred land and haven for refuge and healing
So chaste but peculiar and legendary
Yet purely favoured in its traditional white regalia
This bilingual coastal county with breathtaking scenarios
Overlooking the ever sweating Atlantic Ocean
Opens in awe with the greenery of its mountains and slopes
And abounds in flora and fauna

This once all-white megalopolis unfurls
Safeguarding the meek and homeless
And shielding from the storms of life
This bolthole and port in the storm of the iniquitous and depraved
Opens to diversities in all shades, ages and ethnicities
Providing liberty and license to prerogatives
A voice to the voiceless and hope to the hopeless
Immunity from torture and arrests for common humanity
Rest and hospitality from pursuits and hostilities
Generously offering a serene abode, shelter and sustenance
To those fleeing unjust persecution and human rights abuses

This waterfront location with great towers and leisure centres
And the most beautiful doorstep beaches
Medieval castles, golfclubs and waterfalls
A great shopping destination for high street favourites

Miles of shoreline, sand dunes, rock pools and secluded wildlife havens
Beaches with high and very active tides
Gold sands, seaside perfections and medieval castles
Rolling hills, water catchment areas and world class museums
Temperate and unpredictable weather all year round
A rich setting for cultural highlights and lakeside lunch with the swans
Great urban lifestyles, home of the best festivals
Craft shops, parks and proms, art galleries
Massive football stadium, home of the Swans, great musical lyrics
Popular parks and gardens, and other touristic attractions

This fortress and place of rejuvenation and revival
Is home and hope to asylum seekers and refugees
Who have journeyed with a rich repertoire of knowledge and skills

Swansea has given them a sense of belonging and identity
Has welcomed their diversities and flexibilities
Given solace from life's threatening experiences
They have journeyed from far and wide
In trauma, danger and pain
Escaping the wrath and afflictions of humanity
Yearning for peace, safety and refuge
All clad in tales of trafficking, exploitation,
Xenophobia, racism, torture, discrimination
For sexual orientations and different forms of biases
Hideous traditional practices, gender inequality, abuse, political unrest
Armed conflicts, corruption, nepotism, wars and genocide

Swansea is home away from home to the asylum seekers
This City and County offers a wide range of opportunities
With the best charities, community centres, social clubs
Motivational networks and free local services
Accessible refugee organisations and volunteering opportunities
An inclusive approach to refugees, turning their support into
    practical help
Issuing sanctuary awards, scholarships and refugee employment
    workshops
Scrapping hostile environments and binning deportation plans
Fostering Swansea Asylum Seekers Support projects
For a Better Welcome to Swansea

In Swansea, refugees relish a wide range of benefits
Open food and clothes banks, free medical services
Volunteering and study opportunities for everyone
Open University and Sanctuary scholarships
Sanctuary schools, holistic care and helplines
Free English lessons and educational support services
Asylum advocacy forums
Many drop-in sessions, outdoors and indoors activities for all ages
Crafts and arts sessions, free computer lessons
Skill development workshops, excursions and some summer free
    bus services

Like Oliver Twist, we must ask for more
For the asylum seeker to feel at home and enjoy full inclusion in
    Swansea
The government still has much to do
Quicker decisions on asylum claims, the right to claim benefits

Jobs for asylum seekers and not just a weekly stipend of £45
Opportunities for asylum seekers to work and pay taxes and improve the community
A fully inclusive agenda in all government sectors and spheres of influence
Equal life opportunities and full support systems
Full refugee involvement in educational forums and policy meetings
Better arrangements and support for asylum seekers with children in schools
Greater participation and full involvement in government
A reduction in bus fares for asylum seekers and free bus services for all children
Amelioration of the living conditions of all asylum seekers and refugees

A cure to this sick and ever evolving world is unconditional love and kindness
Only a City of Sanctuary like Swansea can do it best

When Trees Fall on Trees: Closing Chords

The Fronts Bend

Oh! in our proud prime
The chorus of youthfulness
Amidst the chaos of life
The stunts and the glares
The passage of rites and fantasies
Every dream glows
As tomorrow is not questioned
In this hotness of heads
The blood so active
This trunk is enslaved
Toiling in glamour and pain

Oh! but the tides do change
The rhetorics so vague
Rhythms and lyrics anew
When reality dawns
And we are glued
To quest insatiably
The finest of humanity
Compelled to reap
In solo to the same tune

Now the drummer's weary
The wrinkles so glaring
The fading lights so visible
Resigned to fate
To meekness and illness

This bodily abode so tall
Becomes a caricature
Adieu to melodies
That once woke a stiff limb
May this change be not
A definition of sorrow
But an echo of glories
Of the past and present

Burst Bubbles

Oh! these crooked lines
Go deep in the fabric of our existence
Defining the very essence of our being
The mysteries of our lives

Each second draws nigh
Our steps to the tomb
Echoing our mortal tunes
Awakening our urge for celestial bliss

This weakened wrinkled mass
That boasted and shone of youth
Is tomorrow's filth
And food for the worms

May I be no ingrate
To tear this orb's tale
But quit tearing
For I came in tears

When Trees Fall on Trees

As sunken jaws explode
And heads grow bigger
Weariness hits the limbs
And worries our plagues

This dungeon seems fairer
With maiden tale so weird
The universe seems exhausted
For man's dignity is wanting

What glory is left
In toilers that crawl
The surface of the earth
Scooping for dung

Drained of wit
Resigned to faithlessness
Yet resolved to seek
The pleasures of doom

This surface bestows
More pain than gain
Let my travels be not in vain
For my song has been my pain

If Love Were Human...

Love's face would glow forever
And smiles would brighten the earth
No hands would work all day
To nurture and for nature

All heads would dream of peace
And a world free for all
All hearts would leap for love
And work for peace alone

No blood would ever be shed
Love's feet would be still as mountains
To carry the world as one
If love were truly human

No tears would fill an eye
No pain would cause us fear
All hands would always hug
The young and comfort the meek

All lips would be as smooth
As petals of a tulip
All mouths would profess love
No boundaries would exist

No hatred would prevail
For life's woes would be crushed
Love's body would be perfect
If love were truly human

Printed and bound by CPI Group (UK) Ltd, Croydon, CR0 4YY
29/11/2023
03601451-0001